A Brief Overview of Banks:

Their Past, Present and Future

Bob Navarro

2017

Dedicated to my Angel, Espy

Contents

Introduction

Overview

The history of banks started with the first prototype banks of merchants of the ancient world, which made grain loans to farmers and traders who carried goods between cities. This began around 2000 BCE in Assyria and Babylonia. Later, in ancient Greece and during the Roman Empire, lenders based in temples made loans and added two important innovations: they accepted deposits and they changed money.

However, the crucial development of a banking system began in medieval and Renaissance Italy, in particular, in the cities of Florence, Venice and Genoa. The Bardi and Peruzzi families dominated banking in 14th century Florence, establishing branches in many other parts of Europe. The most famous Italian bank was the Medici bank, established by Giovanni Medici in 1397.

The development of banking spread from northern Italy throughout the Holy Roman Empire, and in the 15th and 16th century to northern Europe. This was followed by a number of important innovations that took place in Amsterdam, Holland, then during the 17th century in the Dutch Republic, and in London, England in the 18th century, especially by the Rothschild family.

During the 20th century, developments in telecommunications and computing caused major changes to banks' operations and allowed banks to increase in size and geographic spread. The Great Depression of 1929 caused many banks to fail, and instituted many laws to regulate banking. The financial crisis that took place between 2007 and 2008 also caused many bank failures, including some of the world's largest banks, and created much debate about imposing more bank regulations. This is particularly true of Goldman-Sachs, which is the world's most powerful investment bank—especially since it was very heavily involved in the 2007-2008 financial crisis.

At present, mobile banking has become the norm for customer touch point banking services, with mobile banking having increased fivefold in a very short period of time. This growth will see a shift in mobile banking operations as they continue to add more functionalities and newer features in their mobile banking solutions. The personal finance management tools (PFM) are now being placed in a prominent place in the online banking site so that customers get to know about what new services are available. Regional banks are institutions, which are trying to make PFM online work in tandem. The introduction of message centers on a widespread basis is also needed. These are dedicated web portals that are designed for secure communication between a bank and its customers. And, tablet banking requires upgrades to allow transactions such as remote deposit captures.

In the future, banks are seriously considering the implementation of digital money—and moving away from cash. This will alter everything that we have known about finance.

The Earliest Banks

Mesopotamia

Banking as an archaic activity is thought to have begun at various times between 4000 and 3000 BCE. Around 2200 BCE, the occurrence of trade was limited to the internal boundaries of each city-state of Babylon and the temple, which was located at the center of economic activity, especially since trade for citizens external to the city was forbidden.

In Babylonia, people depositing gold were required to pay amounts as much as one-sixtieth of the total deposited. Both the palaces and temple are known to have provided lending and issuing from the wealth they held, with the palaces to a lesser extent. Such loans involved issuing seed-grain, with re-payment from the harvest. These basic social agreements were documented in clay tablets, with an agreement on interest accrual. The process of depositing and storing of wealth in temples continued until 200 BCE. Cuneiform records in Babylonia describe financial activities as having occurred sometime after 1000 BC, with economic activities similar to a degree to modern deposit banking—including the provision of credit.

Greece

The city-states of Greece after the Persian Wars produced a government and culture sufficiently organized for the birth of a private citizenship and therefore an embryonic capitalist society, allowing for the separation of wealth from exclusive state ownership to the possibility of ownership by the individual. Trapezites were the first to trade using money, during the 5th century BCE as opposed to earlier trade which occurred using forms of pre-money.

The earliest forms of storage utilized were the rudimentary money boxes, which were made similar to the construction of a bee-hive. Private and civic entities within ancient Grecian society, especially Greek temples, performed financial transactions. The temples were the places where treasure was deposited for safe-keeping. These transactions consisted of deposits, currency exchange, validation of coinage, and loans.

Around 300 BCE, state depositories replaced temples as the location of security deposits. As the need for new buildings to house banking operations increased, construction of these places within the cities began around the courtyards of the markets. Thirty-five Hellenistic cities included private banks during the 2nd century.

Many loans are recorded in writings from the classical age, although a very small proportion were provided by banks. Provision of these were likely an occurrence of Athens, with loans known to have been provided at some time at an annual interest of 12 percent. Within the boundaries of Athens, banker loans are recorded as having been issued. Banks sometimes made loans available confidentially by providing funds without being publicly known. In addition, they acted as intermediaries for persons to loan their own monies without this being known to others.

Egypt

In the 18th century BCE, amounts of gold were deposited within the boundaries of the temple buildings of Egypt for reasons of security. Grain having an intrinsic value as food functioned, in addition to precious metals, as money. The regional granaries were used to store and loan the grain of communities—functions similar to banking services although not the same. The numerous scattered government granaries were transformed into a network of grain banks, which were centralized in Alexandria where the main accounts from all the state granary banks were recorded.

This centralized administration was the first known governmental bank, functioning as a trade credit system that transferred payments between accounts without passing money. There were 2 types of banks operating within Egypt: royal and private. From 300 BCE to 600 CE, banks were of three types: privately run, leased, or owned by government.

Rome

Roman banking activities were an economic situation which had a crucial presence within temples, such as the minting of coins. But, public deposits gradually ceased to be held in temples, and instead were held in private depositories. Around 350 BCE a rudimentary public bank was formed to deal with debt in the impoverished lower classes.

Deposit bankers and banking houses consisted of money lenders who would set up their stalls in the middle of enclosed courtyards on a long bench called a *bancu*, from which the word *bank* is derived. As a moneychanger, the merchant did not so much invest money as merely convert the foreign currency into the only legal tender in Rome—that of the Imperial Mint.

Rental monies were collected from persons using land belonging to a temple and given to the temple treasurer, and banks were obliged to pay its' clients debts under guarantee. State banks were established that were funded by the sale of all the properties owned at the time by the state.

The Roman empire formalized the administrative aspect of banking and instituted greater regulation of financial institutions and financial practices. Charging interest on loans and paying interest on deposits became more highly developed and competitive. The development of Roman banks was limited, however, by the Roman preference for cash transactions. There was also a temporary breakdown of the Roman banking system after the banks rejected the flakes of copper produced by his mints. With the ascent of Christianity, banking became subject to additional restrictions, as the charging of interest was viewed as being immoral. After the fall of Rome, banking temporarily ended in Europe and was not revived until the time of the crusades.

Asia

The temple of Artemis was the largest depository of Asia. During the time at the cessation of the first Mithridatic war the entire debt record was annulled by the council. Mark Anthony stole from the deposits on an occasion.

India

In ancient India there is evidence of loans beginning in 1750 BCE. From 321 to 185 BCE, an instrument called adesha was in use, which was an order on a banker desiring him to pay the money of the note to a third person, which is a bill of exchange. Merchants in large towns gave letters of credit to one another.

China

In ancient China, starting around 200 BCE, Chinese currency developed with the introduction of standardized coins that allowed easier trade across China, and led to development of letters of credit. These letters were issued by merchants who acted in ways that today we would understand as banks.

Medieval Europe

The original banks were those that Italian grain merchants invented in the Middle Ages. As merchants and bankers grew in stature based on cereal crops, many displaced Jews fleeing Spanish persecution were attracted to the trade. They brought with them ancient practices from the Middle and Far East. Originally intended to finance long trading journeys, they applied these methods to finance grain production and trading.

Jews could not hold land in Italy, so they entered the great trading piazzas and halls, alongside local traders, and set up their benches to trade in crops. They had one great advantage over the locals. Christians were strictly forbidden the sin of usury. The Jewish could lend to farmers against crops in the field, a high-risk loan with usurious rates, but the Jews were not subject to the Church's dictates. They could secure the grain-sale rights against the eventual harvest, and began to advance payment against the future delivery of grain shipped to distant ports, making their profit from the present discount against the future price. This two-handed trade was time-consuming and soon there arose a class of merchants who were trading grain debt instead of grain.

The Jewish trader performed both credit and insurance functions. Credit financing took the form of a crop loan at the beginning of the growing season, which allowed a farmer to cultivate his annual crop. Insurance underwriting in the form of a crop, or commodity, guaranteed the delivery of the crop to its buyer. In addition, traders performed the merchant function by making arrangements to supply the buyer of the crop through alternative sources in the event of crop failure. They could also keep the farmer or other commodity producer in business during a drought or other crop failure through the issuance of a crop or commodity insurance against the hazard of failure of his crop.

Merchant banking progressed from financing trade on one's own behalf to settling trades for others and then to holding deposits for settlement of notes written by the people who were still brokering the actual grain. And so the merchant's benches (*banca)* in the great grain markets became centers for holding money against a bill. These deposited funds were intended to be held for the settlement of grain trades, but often were used for the bench's own trades in the meantime. The term bankrupt comes from the phrase *banca rotta*, or broken bench, which is what happened when someone lost his traders' deposits.

In the 12th century, the need to transfer large sums of money to finance the Crusades stimulated the re-emergence of banking in western Europe. In 1162, King Henry II of England levied a tax to support the crusades. The Templars and Hospitallers acted as King Henry's bankers in the Holy Land. The Templars' wide flung, large land holdings across Europe emerged between 1100 and 1300 as the beginning of Europe-wide banking, especially as their practice was to take in local currency, for which a demand note would be given that would be good at any of their castles across Europe, thus allowing the movement of money without the usual risk of robbery while traveling.

A manner of discounting interest to the depositors against what could be earned by employing their money in the trade of the bench was developed. Selling an interest to them in a specific trade overcame the usury objection by developing a method of financing the long-distance transport of goods. Medieval trade fairs contributed to the growth of banking, with moneychangers issuing documents redeemable at other fairs in exchange for hard currency. These documents could be cashed at another fair in a different country or at a future fair in the same location. If redeemable at a future date, they would often be discounted by an amount comparable to a rate of interest. Eventually, these documents evolved into bills of exchange, which could be redeemed at any office of the issuing banker. These bills made it possible to transfer large sums of money without the complications of hauling large chests of gold and hiring armed guards to protect the gold from thieves.

In 1156, in Genoa, Italy, the earliest known foreign exchange contract occurred. Two brothers borrowed 115 Genoese pounds and agreed to reimburse the bank's agents in Constantinople the sum of 460 bezants one month after their arrival in that city. In the following century the use of such contracts grew rapidly, particularly since profits from time differences were seen as not infringing canon laws against usury.

The Beginnings of Modern Banking

The Italian Bankers

Modern banking is traceable to early Renaissance Italy, especially to rich cities such as Florence, Venice and Genoa. The first bank to be established was in Venice with guarantee from the State in 1157. This was due to the commercial agency of the Venetians, acting in the interest of the Crusaders of Pope Urban the Second, due to costs of the expansion of the empire, and to relieve the subsequent financial burden on the republic.

The Chamber of Loans, was created to manage the affairs of loans, with repayment at 4 percent interest. Changes in the enterprises of the Chamber, firstly by the commencing of use of discounting exchanges and later by the receipt of deposits, there developed the functioning of the organization into the Bank of Venice, with an initial capital of 5,000,000 ducats. Banking practice began in the 12th century, and continued until the bank ceased to operate during the French invasion of 1797. There were several banking failures during this time.

In the 13th century, groups of Italian Christians invented legal fictions to get around the ban on Christian usury. One method of effecting a loan with interest was to offer money without interest, but to require that the loan was insured against possible loss or injury, or delays in repayment. Then, a distinction evolved between things that were consumable, such as food and fuel, and those that were not, with usury permitted on loans that involved the latter. By 1327, Avignon, France had 43 branches of Italian banking houses. The growth of Italian banking in France was the start of the Lombard moneychangers in Europe, who moved from city to city along the busy pilgrim routes important for trade.

The most powerful banking families came from Florence, including the Acciaiuoli, Bardi and Peruzzi families, which established branches in many other parts of Europe. By 1338, there were more than 80 banking houses in Florence. The most famous Italian bank was the Medici bank.

The Peruzzi Bankers

The Peruzzi were bankers of Florence, Italy, and were among the leading families of the city in the 14th century before the rise of the Medici family. Their beginnings stretch back to the 11th century. A restructuring of the Peruzzi company in 1300, with an infusion of outside capital, marked the start of 25 years of prosperity that brought the family to the forefront of Florentine affairs. Semi-public patronage reaffirmed the Peruzzi status in Florence. The surviving account books of the Peruzzi provide an economic history of the city.

The company that bore the Peruzzi name was run by a half-dozen family members. The company's courier system acted as an intelligence-gathering system that was often embroiled in diplomacy. By 1330, the Peruzzi bank was the second largest in Europe, with 15 branches from the Middle East to London, all capitalized to the sum of more than 100,000 gold florins. Trade beyond Italy required agents and instruments of credit, and this extended the family business into an international network. The development of the double-entry bookkeeping made such complicated financial transactions possible. By the 14th century, the main activity of the Peruzzi had switched to wholesale commodities trading on a very large scale, especially in grain—for which they were granted a monopoly— and to banking, in which popes, nobles, bourgeois, towns and abbeys drew loans from the Peruzzi. In 1343 the Peruzzi consortium collapsed and was bankrupt in 1345, with their partners in risk-capital, the Bardi. Not all of the family fortunes were lost in the bankruptcy, and the Peruzzi continued to be among the prominent families of Florence.

The Bardi Bankers

The Bardi family were an influential Florentine family that started a powerful banking company in 1164. During the 14th century the Bardi family became so powerful that the Florentine government considered them a threat. They eventually were forced to sell their castle to Florence because fortified castles near the city were seen as a danger to the republic.

In 1290, the Bardi and Peruzzi families established branches in England, and were the main European bankers by 1320. By the 14th century the Bardi and the Peruzzi family grew very wealthy by offering financial services. These two families facilitated trade by providing the merchants with bills of exchange. Thus, the money paid by a debtor in one town could be paid out to creditor just by presenting the bill in another town. The Bardi family had 13 different branches located in Barcelona, Seville and Majorca, Spain; in Paris, Avignon, Nice, Bruges and Marseilles, France; in London, England; in Constantinople of the Roman/Byzantine Empire; in Rhodes and Cypress, Greece; and in Jerusalem, Palestine.

During the Hundred Years War starting in 1337, King Edward III of England was engaged in an expensive war with France. He borrowed 600,000 gold florins from the Peruzzi banking family and another 900,000 gold florins from the Bardi family. In 1345, King Edward III defaulted on his payments, causing both banking families to go bankrupt. Despite the failure of the bank, the Bardi family remained successful merchants. The marriage of a Bardi daughter to a Medici in 1415 was a key factor in establishing the House of Medici in power in Florence. The Bardi family was rewarded for its support by restoring their political rights in 1434, and in 1444, they were exempted from paying particular taxes. During the 15th century the Bardi family continued to operate in various European centers, playing a notable role in financing some of the early voyages of discovery to America, including those by Christopher Columbus and John Cabot.

The Acciaioli Bankers

The Acciaioli was an important family of Florence that began in 1160, and founded a powerful bank in the 13th century, which had branches from Greece to Western Europe.

Later they associated themselves to the Albizzi family and then to the Medici family in the 15th century. From 1390 to 1460 they ruled the Duchy of Athens, and kept close ties with the Medici family through the marriage of a daughter to a Medici.

In 1401 the magistrates of Barcelona, Spain established the first replication of the Venetian model of exchange and deposit—the Table of Exchange. In 1407, the Bank of Saint George was founded in Genoa, Italy and dominated business in the Mediterranean. In the 1500s, the Genoese people produced a number of important banking family groups. The Grimaldi, Spinola, Pallavicino, Doria, Pinelli and Lomellini families were especially influential and wealthy.

In 1400, political forces turned against the Italian bankers, and in 1401, King Martin I of Aragon, Spain had some of these bankers expelled. In 1403, King Henry IV of England prohibited the Italian bankers from taking profits in any way in his kingdom. In 1409, Flanders imprisoned and then expelled Genoese bankers. In 1410, all Italian merchants were expelled from Paris, France.

The Medici Family

The House of Medici was an Italian banking family that first began to gather prominence under in Florence during the first half of the 15th century. The family originated in the Tuscan countryside, gradually rising until they were able to fund the Medici Bank. The bank was the largest in Europe during the 15th century, and gained political power in Florence.

The Medici wealth and influence initially derived from the textile trade. Like other signore families, they dominated their city's government, and they were able to bring Florence under their family's power. In doing so, they created an environment where art and humanism could flourish. They along with other families of Italy, fostered and inspired the birth of the Italian Renaissance.

The Medici Bank was one of the most prosperous and most respected institutions in Europe. The Medici family was the wealthiest family in Europe for a time, and they acquired political power in Florence and in wider Italy and Europe. A notable contribution to the profession of accounting was the improvement of the general ledger system through the development of the double-entry bookkeeping system for tracking credits and debits

Until the late 14th century the leading family of Florence was the House of Albizzi. In 1293 the Ordinances of Justice were enacted, which effectively became the constitution of the republic of Florence throughout the Italian Renaissance. The city's numerous luxurious palazzi were surrounded by townhouses built by the merchant class.In 1298, one of the leading banking families of Europe, the Bonsignoris, were bankrupted, so the city of Siena its status as the banking center of Europe to Florence.

The main challengers of the Albizzi family were the Medicis. The Medici family controlled the Medici bank—then Europe's largest bank—and an array of other enterprises in Florence and elsewhere. In 1433, the Albizzi managed to have Cosimo Medici exiled. In 1434, however, a pro-Medici Signoria was elected and Cosimo returned. The Medici became the city's leading family, a position they would hold for the next 3 centuries. The republican government was under the control of the Medici and their allies, even though the Medicis rarely held official posts, but were nevertheless the unquestioned leaders. Members of the Medici family rose to prominence in the early 14th century in the wool trade. Despite the presence of some Medici in the city's government institutions, they were still far less notable than families such as the Albizzi and Strozzi. Three successive generations of the Medici ruled over Florence through the greater part of the 15th century, without abolishing the representative government, but clearly dominating it. In the 16th century the Medici family was able to rule until 1537.

However, the Medici remained masters of Italy through the 16th century popes, Leo X and Clement VII, who were *de facto* rulers of both Rome and Florence. In the 17th century they retained their power through Pope Paul V and Pope Urban VIII. It wasn't until the 18th century that the Medici dynasty finally fell from power.

Arabic Banking

In the 16th century, the leading financiers in Istanbul were the Greeks and Jews. Many of the Jewish financiers were Marranos who had fled from Iberia during the period leading up to the expulsion of Jews from Spain. Some of these families brought great fortunes with them, and the most notable of the Jewish banking families in the 16th century Ottoman Empire was the Marrano banking house of Mendes, which moved to Istanbul in 1552, under the protection of Sultan Suleyman the Magnificent. When Alvaro Mendes arrived in Istanbul in the Ottoman Empire in 1588, he brought with him 85,000 gold ducats. The Mendes family then acquired a dominating position in the state finances of the Ottoman Empire and in commerce with Europe. They also thrived in Baghdad, Iraq during the 18th and 19th centuries under the Ottoman Empire, performing commercial functions such as moneylending and banking. The Jews could engage in commercial activities, such as moneylending and banking, which were proscribed for Muslims under Islamic law.

Court Jews

Court Jews were Jewish bankers who lent money and handled the finances of some of the Christian European noble houses in the 17th and 18th centuries. Their jobs included raising revenues by tax farming, negotiating loans, master of the mint, creating new sources for revenue, floating debentures, devising new taxes. and supplying the military. In addition, the Court Jews acted as personal bankers for nobility: they raised money to cover the nobles' personal diplomacy and extravagances.

Court Jews were skilled administrators and businessmen who received privileges in return for their services. They were found in Germany, Holland, Austria, Denmark, England, Hungary, Italy, Poland, Lithuania, Portugal, and Spain. Virtually every duchy, principality, and palatinate in the Holy Roman Empire had a Court Jew.

Germany

In the southern German realm, two great banking families emerged in the 15th century, the Fuggers and the Welsers. They controlled much of the European economy and dominated international high finance in the 16th century. Dutch bankers also played a central role in establishing banking in the Northern German city states. Berenberg Bank was established in 1590 by Dutch brothers Hans and Paul Berenberg in Hamburg, Germany.

Holland

Throughout the 17th century, precious metals from the New World, Japan and other places were being channeled into Europe, with corresponding price increases. Thanks to the free coinage, the Bank of Amsterdam, and the heightened trade and commerce, the Netherlands attracted much coin and bullion to be deposited in their banks. These concepts of fractional-reserve banking and payment systems were further developed and spread to England.

England

London, England did not have any banking houses operating until the 17th century, although the London Royal Exchange was established in 1565. Wealthy merchants began to store their gold with the goldsmiths of London, who possessed private vaults and charged a fee for their service. In exchange for each deposit of precious metal, the goldsmiths issued receipts certifying the quantity and purity of the metal that they held. These receipts could not be assigned because only the original depositor could collect the stored goods.

The goldsmiths began to lend the money out on behalf of the depositor, which led to the development of modern banking practices. Promissory notes, which evolved into banknotes, were issued for money deposited as a loan to the goldsmith. These practices created a new kind of money that was actually debt, rather than silver or gold coin, a commodity that had been regulated and controlled by the monarchy. This development required the acceptance in trade of the goldsmiths' promissory notes, payable on demand. Acceptance in turn required a general belief that coin would be available, and a fractional reserve served for this purpose. Acceptance also required that the holders of debt be able to enforce an unconditional right to payment. It required that the notes, as well as drafts, be negotiable instruments. Nevertheless, an act of Parliament was required in the early 18th century to overrule court decisions holding that the goldsmiths' notes, despite the customs of merchants, were not negotiable.

The Emergence of Modern Banking

The Evolution of Banking

By the end of the 16th century and during the 17th century, the traditional banking functions of accepting deposits, moneylending, money changing and transferring funds were combined with the issuance of bank debt that served as a substitute for gold and silver coins. New banking practices promoted commercial and industrial growth by providing a safe and convenient means of payment and a money supply more responsive to commercial needs, as well as by discounting business debt. By the end of the 17th century, banking was also becoming important for the funding requirements of the combative European states. This would lead on to government regulations and the first central banks.

The Modern Bank

The first bank to begin the permanent issue of banknotes was the Bank of England in 1695. Initially hand-written and issued on deposit or as a loan, they promised to pay the bearer the value of the note on demand. By 1745, standardized printed notes ranging from 20 to 1,000 English pounds were being printed. Fully printed notes that didn't require the name of the payee and the cashier's signature first appeared in 1855.

The rise of Protestantism freed many European Christians from Rome's dictates against usury. In the 18th century, services offered by banks increased. Clearing facilities, security investments, cheques and overdraft protections were introduced. Cheques were invented in the 1600s in England and banks settled payments by direct courier to the issuing bank. Around 1770, they began meeting in a central location, and by the 1800s a dedicated space was established, known as a banker's clearing house. The London clearing house used a method where each bank paid cash to and then was paid cash by an inspector at the end of each day. The first overdraft facility was set up in 1728 by the Royal Bank of Scotland.

The Industrial Revolution and growing international trade increased the number of banks, especially in London. New types of financial activities broadened the scope of banking from underwriting bonds to originating foreign loans. These new merchant banks facilitated trade growth, profiting from England's emerging dominance in seaborne shipping. Two immigrant families, Rothschild and Baring, established merchant banking firms in London in the late 18th century and came to dominate world banking in the 19th century.

A great impetus to country banking came in 1797 when England was threatened by war, and the Bank of England suspended cash payments. A handful of Frenchmen landed in Pembrokeshire, England, causing a panic. Shortly after this incident, the English Parliament authorized the Bank of England and country bankers to issue notes of low denomination.

Japanese Banking

Modern banking began during a period between 1868 to WWI. The beginning of the Meiji government's attempts at formulating a functioning banking system started in 1868, and continued until 1881. The Imperial mint was begun using imported machines from Britain during the early years of the Meiji period.

Development of Central Banking

The Bank of Amsterdam became a model for the functioning of a bank for monetary exchange and central banking. An early central bank was the Sveriges Riksbank, which was established in 1668.

In England in the 1690s, public funds were in short supply and were needed to finance the ongoing conflict with France. The credit of King William III's government was very low in London such that it was impossible for it to borrow the 1,200,000 English pounds that the government wanted. In order to induce subscription to the loan, the subscribers were to be incorporated by the name of the Governor and Company of the Bank of England. The bank was given exclusive possession of the government's balances, and was the only limited-liability corporation allowed to issue banknotes. The lenders would give the government bullion, and also issue notes against the government bonds, which could then be lent again.

The establishment of the Bank of England, the model on which most modern central banks have been based on, was devised by Earl Charles Montagu in 1694. He proposed a loan of 1,200,000 English pounds to the government. In return, the subscribers would be incorporated as *The Governor and Company of the Bank of England* with long-term banking privileges, including the issuance of notes. The Royal Charter was granted in 1694 through the passage of the Tonnage Act. Although the bank was originally a private institution, by the end of the 18th century it was being regarded as a public authority with civic responsibility toward the upkeep of a healthy financial system. The currency crises in 1797, which was caused by panicked depositors withdrawing from the bank, led to the government suspending convertibility of notes into specie payment. The bank was accused by the bullionists of causing the exchange rate to fall from over issuing banknotes.

Henry Thornton is regarded as the father of the modern central bank. An opponent of the real bills doctrine, he was a defender of the bullionist position and a significant figure in monetary theory. In 1802, as a response to the currency crisis, Thornton wrote *An Enquiry into the Nature and Effects of the Paper Credit of Great Britain* in which he argued that the increase in paper credit as a process of monetary expansion did not cause the crisis. The book gave a detailed account of the British monetary system as well as a detailed examination of the ways in which the Bank of England should act to counteract fluctuations in the value of the English pound.

Until the mid-19th century, commercial banks were able to issue their own banknotes, and notes issued by provincial banking companies were commonly in circulation. The origins of the central bank lie with the passage of the Bank Charter Act in 1844. Under this law, authorization to issue new banknotes was restricted to the Bank of England. The act served to restrict the supply of new notes reaching circulation, and gave the Bank of England an effective monopoly on the printing of new notes. The Bank of England accepted the role of lender of last resort in the 1870s after criticism of its lackluster response to the Overend-Gurney Company, which collapsed in 1866, owing about 11,000,000 English pounds.

Central banks were established in many European countries during the 19th century. The War of the Second Coalition led to the creation of the Banque de France in 1800 in an effort to improve the public financing of the war. In 1913, the United States Federal Reserve Bank was created by Congress. Australia established its first central bank in 1920, Colombia in 1923, Mexico in 1925, Chile in 1925, Canada in 1934, and New Zealand in 1934. By 1935, the only significant independent nation that did not possess a central bank was Brazil, which developed one in 1945, and the present central bank in 1965. Having gained independence, African and Asian countries also established central banks or monetary unions.

The Rothschild Family

Overview

The Rothschild family is a wealthy family that flourished in Frankfurt, Germany in the 1760s. The original Rothschild managed to bequeath his wealth and established an international banking family through his five sons, who established themselves in London, England; Paris, France; Frankfurt, Germany; Vienna, Austria; and Naples, Italy. During the 19th century, the Rothschild family possessed the largest private fortune in the world, as well as the largest private fortune in modern world history. The family's wealth was divided among various descendants, and today their interests cover a diverse range of fields, including financial services, real estate, mining, energy, mixed farming, wine and charities.

The Rothschild family's ascent to international prominence began with Mayer Rothschild in Frankfurt, Germany in the 18th century. He was a money changer who developed a finance house and spread his empire by installing each of his five sons in the five main European financial centers. This is why the Rothschild coat of arms contains a clenched fist with five arrows symbolizing the five dynasties established by the five sons of Mayer Rothschild, with the family motto appearing below the shield: *Concordia, Integritas, Industria* (Unity, Integrity, Industry).

The new kind of international bank created by the Rothschilds was impervious to local attacks. Their assets were held in financial instruments, circulating through the world as stocks, bonds and debts. Changes made by the Rothschilds allowed them to insulate their property from local violence so that their real wealth was beyond the reach of any mo— and almost beyond the reach of any monarchs. Their fortune was generated to the greatest extent by Nathan Rothschild in London, England. However, greater and equal profits also were realized by the other Rothschild dynasties, including James Rothschild in Paris, Carl Rothschild in Naples, Italy and Amschel Rothschild in Frankfurt, Germany.

Another essential part of Mayer Rothschild's strategy for future success was to keep control of their banks in family hands, allowing them to maintain full secrecy about the size of their fortunes. The practice initiated by the Rothschilds of having several brothers of a firm establish branches in the different financial centers allowed them to obtain an increasing share of international finance during the 19th century. Mayer Rothschild successfully kept the fortune in the family with carefully arranged marriages, often between first- or second-cousins in a similar manner as for royal intermarriages.

Financing of War

The Rothschilds already possessed a significant fortune before the start of the Napoleonic Wars that took place between 1803 and 1815, and had gained preeminence in the bullion trade. Nathan Rothschild in London was instrumental in almost single-handedly financing the British war effort, organizing the shipment of bullion to the Duke of Wellington's armies across Europe, as well as arranging the payment of British financial subsidies to their continental allies. In 1815, the Rothschilds provided 9,800,000 English pounds in subsidy loans to Britain's continental allies.

Nathan Rothschild calculated that the future reduction in government borrowing brought about by the peace would create a bounce in British government bonds after a two-year stabilization, which would finalize the post-war restructuring of the domestic economy. Nathan Rothschild bought up the government bond market before waiting two years, and then selling the bonds on the crest of a short bounce in the market in 1817 for a 40 percent profit.

The Japanese government also approached the London and Paris families for funding during the Russo-Japanese War that started in 1904. The London consortium's issue of Japanese war bonds totaled 11,500,000 English pounds.

International Financing

In 1818, Nathan Rothschild arranged a loan of 5,000,000 English pounds to the Prussian government. Thus, the issuing of bonds for government loans formed a mainstay of his bank's business. He gained a position of such power in London that by 1826 he was able to supply enough coin to the Bank of England to enable it to avert a market liquidity crisis.

Rothschild family banking businesses pioneered international high finance during the industrialization of Europe and were instrumental in supporting railway systems across the world as well as in complex government financing for projects such as the Suez Canal. During the 19th century, the family bought up a large proportion of the property in Mayfair, London. By the end of the 19th century, the family owned, over 41 palaces of a scale and luxury unparalleled by even the richest royal families.

The Rothschild family was involved in the independence of Brazil from Portugal in the early 19th century. Upon an agreement, the Brazilian government paid a compensation of 2,000,000 pounds sterling to the Kingdom of Portugal to accept Brazil's independence. Thus, the Rothschilds were pre-eminent in raising capital for the government of the Empire of Brazil on the London market. In 1825, Nathan Rothschild raised 2,000,000 English pounds, and was involved in the earlier tranche of this loan which raised 1,000,000 English pounds in 1824. Part of the price of Portuguese recognition of Brazilian independence was that Brazil should take over repayment of the principal and interest on a 1,500,000 English pound loan made to the Portuguese government in 1823 by the Rothschilds.

Modern History

Since the late-19th century, the family Rothschild businesses are on a smaller scale than they were throughout the 19th century, although they encompass a diverse range of fields, including real estate, financial services, wine and charities. Since 2003, a group of Rothschild banks have been controlled by Rothschild Continuation Holdings, a Swiss-registered holding company. 20 percent of Rothschild Continuation Holdings AG was sold in 2005 to Jardine Strategic, a Hong Kong, China entity. In 2008, Rabobank Group of the Netherlands acquired 7½ percent of Rothschild Continuation Holdings AG in a move that was intended to help Rothschild Continuation Holdings AG gain access to a wider capital pool, thus enlarging its presence in East Asian markets.

In 2004, the investment bank of the firm withdrew from the gold market, a commodity the Rothschild bankers had traded in for two centuries. In 2009, Jacob Rothschild invested $200,000,000 in a North Sea Oil company. In 2010, Nathaniel Rothschild bought a substantial share of the Glencore mining and oil company's market capitalization as well as a large share of an aluminum mining company. In 2012, they announced a purchase of a 37 per cent stake in a Rockefeller family wealth advisory and asset management group.

The Bank of England

The Bank of England is the central bank of the United Kingdom and the model on which most modern central banks have been based. Established in 1694, it is the second oldest central bank in operation today, after the Sveriges Riksbank. The Bank's headquarters have been in London since 1734. It was established to act as the English government's banker and was privately owned by stockholders until it was nationalized in 1946. In 1998, it became an independent public organization, wholly owned by the British Treasury Solicitor on behalf of the English government, with independence in setting monetary policy.

The Bank is one of eight banks authorized to issue banknotes in the United Kingdom, but it has a monopoly on the issue of banknotes in England and Wales, and regulates the issue of banknotes by commercial banks in Scotland and Northern Ireland. The Bank's Monetary Policy Committee has a responsibility for managing monetary policy. The British Treasury has reserve powers to give orders to the committee if they are required in the public interest and by extreme economic circumstances, but such orders must be endorsed by Parliament. The Bank's Financial Policy Committee held its first meeting in 2011 as a macro prudential regulator to oversee regulation of the United Kingdom financial sector. As a regulator and central bank, the Bank of England has not offered consumer banking services for many years, but it still manages some services such as exchanging superseded bank notes. Until 2016, the bank provided personal banking services as a privilege for its employees.

The establishment of the bank in 1694 was devised by Charles Montagu, the 1st Earl of Halifax. He proposed a loan of 1,200,000 English pounds to the government, and in return the subscribers would be incorporated as The Governor and Company of the Bank of England with long-term banking privileges including the issuance of notes. The Royal Charter was granted through the passage of the Tonnage Act in 1694.

When the idea of the national debt came about during the 18th century, this was also managed by the bank. By the charter renewal in 1781, it was also the bankers' bank – keeping enough gold to pay its notes on demand until 1797 when the war between England and France had diminished gold reserves. Following an invasion scare, the government prohibited the bank from paying out in gold by the passing of the Bank Restriction Act in 1797.

In 1844, the Bank Charter Act tied the issue of banknotes to the gold reserves and gave the bank sole rights with regard to their issue. Private banks who previously had that right retained it, provided that their headquarters were outside London and that they deposited security against the banknotes that they issued. A few English banks continued to issue their own notes until the last of them was taken over in the 1930s, although Scottish and Northern Irish private banks still have that right.

Britain remained on the gold standard until 1931, when the gold and foreign exchange reserves were transferred to the English Treasury, but they continued to be managed by the Bank. From 1920 to 1944, the Bank made deliberate efforts to move away from commercial banking and become a central bank. In 1946, the bank was nationalized by Britain. After 1945 the Bank pursued the goals of Keynesian economics, especially easy money and low interest rates to support the aggregate demand. It tried to keep a fixed exchange rate, and attempted to deal with inflation and sterling weakness by credit and exchange controls.

In 1977, the Bank set up a subsidiary, the Bank of England Nominees Limited, with two shareholders: The Bank of England, and the Secretary of the Bank of England. In 1981 the reserve requirement for banks to hold a minimum fixed proportion of their deposits as reserves at the Bank of England was abolished. The bank was also granted operational independence over monetary policy, and under the terms of the Bank of England Act of 1998, the bank's Monetary Policy Committee was given sole responsibility for setting interest rates to meet the English government's inflation target.

Currently, there are two main areas which are handled by the bank to ensure it carries out monetary stability: stable prices and confidence in the currency. The Bank may also act as the lender of last resort by extending credit when no other institution will. The Bank acts as the government's banker, and also manages the country's foreign exchange and gold reserves as well as acting as the bankers' bank. The Bank is custodian to the official gold reserves of the United Kingdom and about 30 other countries. As of 2016, the Bank held around 400,000 bars of gold. These gold deposits were estimated in 2017 to have a current market value of 142,000,000,000 British pounds, with the vault holding 3% of the gold that has been mined throughout human history.

The 20th Century

The first decade of the 20th century saw the Panic of 1907 in the United States, which led to numerous runs on banks, and became known as the bankers' panic. During the Crash of 1929, margin requirements were only 10%. Brokerage firms would lend $9 for every $1 an investor had deposited. When the market fell, brokers called in these loans, which could not be paid back. Banks began to fail as debtors defaulted on debt and depositors attempted to withdraw their deposits, triggering multiple bank runs. Government guarantees and Federal Reserve banking regulations to prevent such panics were ineffective, and bank failures led to the loss of billions of dollars in assets. After the panic of 1929, and during 1930, 744 United States banks failed. By 1933, around $7,000,000,000 in deposits had been frozen in failed banks or in those left unlicensed after the banking holiday was declared by President Franklin Roosevelt.

Bank failures snowballed as desperate bankers called in loans that borrowers did not have time or money to repay. With future profits looking poor, capital investment and construction slowed or completely ceased. In the face of bad loans and worsening future prospects, the surviving banks became even more conservative in their lending. Banks built up their capital reserves and made fewer loans, which intensified deflationary pressures. A cycle developed and the downward spiral accelerated, and over 9,000 banks failed during the 1930s. In response, the United States established the Securities and Exchange Commission (SEC) in 1933, and Congress passed the Glass-Steagall Act, which separated investment banking from commercial banking. This was to avoid risky investment banking activities from ever causing commercial bank failures again.

In the 1980s, global banking and capital market services proliferated after the deregulation of financial markets. Retail banks acquired investment banks and stock brokers created universal banks that offered a wide range of banking services. The trend spread to the United States after much of the Glass-Steagall Act was repealed in the 1980s. This saw United States retail banks embark on a round of mergers and acquisitions, as well as engaging in investment banking activities.

Financial services continued to grow through the 1980s and 1990s as a result of a great increase in demand from companies, governments, and financial institutions. This period saw a significant internationalization of financial markets. The increase of United States foreign investments from Japan not only provided the funds to corporations in the United States, but also helped finance the federal government. The growth of foreign financial markets resulted from large increases in the pool of savings in foreign countries, such as Japan, and from the deregulation of foreign financial markets, which enabled them to expand their activities. Thus, American corporations and banks sought investment opportunities abroad, which prompted the development in the United States of mutual funds specializing in trading in foreign stock markets.

Such growing internationalization and opportunity in financial services changed the competitive landscape, as now many banks would demonstrate a preference for the universal banking model that was prevalent in Europe. Universal banks were free to engage in all forms of financial services, make investments in client companies, and function as much as possible as a one-stop supplier of retail and wholesale financial services.

In 1979, the Federal Reserve System of the United States raised the Discount Rate that it charged its member banks from 9.5% to 12% in an effort to reduce inflation. This had a negative effect on the savings and loans associations (S&Ls), which had issued long-term loans at fixed interest rates that were lower than the interest rate at which they could borrow. In addition, the S&Ls had the liability of the deposits, which paid higher interest rates than the rate at which they could borrow. When interest rates at which they could borrow increased, the S&Ls could not attract adequate capital from deposits to savings accounts of members, and they became insolvent. Rather than admit to insolvency, lax regulatory oversight allowed some S&Ls to invest in highly speculative investment strategies. This had the effect of extending the period where S&Ls were technically insolvent.

This effect created the savings and loan crisis of the 1980s and 1990s in which the failure of 1,043 S&Ls out of the 3,234 in the United States from 1986 to 1995 occurred. The Federal Savings and Loan Insurance Corporation closed or otherwise resolved 296 institutions from 1986 to 1989 and the Resolution Trust Corporation (RTC), which was created to resolve the S&L crisis, closed or otherwise resolved 747 institutions from 1989 to 1995. By 1995, the RTC had closed 747 failed institutions nationwide, worth about $400,000,000,000. In 1996, the GAO estimated the total cost to be $160,000,000,000 to taxpayers.

The Federal Reserve Bank

The Panic of 1907 was headed off by a private conglomerate, led by J. P. Morgan, who set themselves up as lenders of last resort to banks that were in trouble. This effort succeeded in stopping the panic, and led to calls for a Federal agency to do the same thing. In response to this, the Federal Reserve System was created by Congress in 1913, establishing a new central bank intended to serve as a formal lender of last resort to banks in times of liquidity crisis panics where depositors tried to withdraw their money faster than a normal fractional-reserve-based bank could pay it out.

The Federal Reserve Act by Congress allowed for a regional Federal Reserve System, operating under a supervisory board in Washington, D.C. The Act provided for the establishment of Federal Reserve Banks, to furnish an elastic currency, to afford means of rediscounting commercial paper, to establish a more effective supervision of banking in the United States, and for other purposes. The Act provided for a Reserve Bank Organization Committee that would designate no less than eight but no more than twelve cities to be Federal Reserve cities, and would then divide the nation into districts, each district to contain one Federal Reserve City. The legislation also provided for a system that included a number of regional Federal Reserve Banks and a seven-member governing board. All national banks were required to join the system and other banks could also join.

In 1914, the Reserve Bank Organization Committee announced the establishment of twelve Federal Reserve banks to cover various districts throughout the country. Initially, this bank's influence was restricted to New York State, with over $20,000,000 in capital stock being invested. As a result, the New York Fed became the largest and most dominant bank in the system. The Bank took in $100,000,000 from 211 member banks on its first day, made two rediscounts, and received its first shipment of Federal Reserve Notes. The Federal Reserve System, of which the twelve regional Federal Reserve banks are a part, was created by Congress in 1913 in a response to a series of economic crises at the turn of the early 20th century. By 1927, the bank contained 10% of the world's entire store of monetary gold.

The Fed is an independent financial institution formed within the United States, that works separately from the executive or judicial branches of government. The Federal Reserve System is considered to be an independent agency that exists outside of the cabinet of the executive and its powers are derived directly from Congress. Over the past century, the Federal Reserve Bank's power has expanded from its original roles such as a private response to problems in banking systems and establishing a more effective supervisory role of banking systems in the United States to its now current position of being a lender of last resort to banking institutions that require additional credit to stay afloat.

The twelve regional Federal Reserve Banks were established as the operating arms of the nation's central banking system. They are organized much like private corporations, with some features of private corporations and some features of public federal agencies. The

United States has an interest in the Federal Reserve Banks as tax-exempt federally created instrumentalities whose profits belong to the federal government, but this interest is not proprietary. The Reserve Banks are not federal instrumentalities, but are independent, privately owned and locally controlled corporations. The Federal Reserve System provides the government with a ready source of loans and serves as the safe depository for federal money. The Federal Reserve is also a low-cost mechanism for transferring funds and is an inexpensive agent for meeting payments on the national debt and government salaries.

The Federal Reserve Banks issue shares of stock to member banks. However, owning Federal Reserve Bank stock is quite different from owning stock in a private company. The Federal Reserve Banks are not operated for profit, and ownership of a certain amount of stock is, by law, a condition of membership in the system. The stock may not be sold or traded or pledged as security for a loan. By law, dividends are limited to 6% per year. The dividends paid to member banks are considered partial compensation for the lack of interest paid on member banks' required reserves held at the Federal Reserve. By law, banks in the United States must maintain fractional reserves, most of which are kept on account at the Federal Reserve. The Federal Reserve does not pay interest on these funds, although it has authority granted by Congress to pay interest on these funds.

A major responsibility of The Federal Reserve is to oversee their banking and financial systems. Maintaining confidence in the soundness of the banking and financial systems is what mobilizes a society's savings, allows the savings to be channeled into productive investments, and encourages economic growth. Each Federal Reserve Bank funds its own operations, primarily from interest on its loans and on the securities it holds. Expenses and dividends paid are typically a small fraction of a Federal Reserve Bank's revenue each year. By law the remainder must be transferred to the Board of Governors, which then deposits the full amount to the Treasury as interest on outstanding Federal Reserve Notes.

The Federal Reserve Banks conduct ongoing internal audits of their operations to ensure that their accounts are accurate and comply with the Federal Reserve System's accounting principles. The banks are also subject to two types of external auditing. The GAO) conducts regular audits of the banks' operations. The GAO audits are reported to the public, but they may not review a bank's monetary policy decisions or disclose them to the public. Each bank is required to submit to an annual audit by an external accounting firm, which produces a confidential report to the bank and a summary statement for the bank's annual report. Some members of Congress want a more intrusive GAO audit of the Federal Reserve System, but Federal Reserve representatives support the existing restrictions to prevent political influence over long-range economic decisions.

The Federal Reserve contains 12 Districts in the following 12 cities of the United States:

- Boston, Massachusetts

- New York City, New York

- Philadelphia, Pennsylvania

- Cleveland, Ohio

- Richmond, Virginia

- Atlanta, Georgia

- Chicago, Illinois

- St. Louis, Missouri

- Minneapolis, Minnesota

- Kansas City, Missouri

- Dallas, Texas

- San Francisco, California

The World Bank

During the post-WWII period and with the introduction of the Bretton Woods System in 1944, two organizations were created: The International Monetary Fund (IMF) and the World Bank Group (WBG). Encouraged by these institutions, commercial banks started to lend to sovereign states in the third world. When the gold standard was abandoned in 1971, a number of the banks became bankrupt due to third world country debt defaults.

In 1959, banks agreed on a standard for machine readable characters for use with cheques, which led to the first automated reader-sorter machines. In the 1960s, the first Automated Teller Machines (ATMs) were developed and the first machines started to appear by the end of the decade. Banks started to become heavy investors in computer technology to automate much of the manual processing, which began a shift by banks from large clerical staffs to new automated systems. By the 1970s the first payment systems started to develop that would lead to electronic payment systems for both international and domestic payments. The international SWIFT payment network was established in 1973 and domestic payment systems were developed around the world by banks working together with governments.

The WBG was established in 1944 to rebuild post-WWII Europe under the International Bank for Reconstruction and Development (IBRD). Currently, the WBG functions as an international organization that fights poverty by offering developmental assistance to middle-income and low-income countries. By giving loans and offering advice and training in both the private and public sectors, the WBG aims to eliminate poverty by helping people help themselves. Under the WBG, there are complimentary institutions that aid in its goals to provide assistance.

There are 184 member countries that are shareholders in the IBRD, which is the primary arm of the WBG. To become a member, however, a country must first join the IMF. The size of the WBG's shareholders, like that of the IMF's shareholders, depends on the size of a country's economy. Thus, the cost of a subscription to the WBG is a factor of the quota paid to the IMF. There is also an obligatory subscription fee, which is equivalent to almost 90% of the quota that a country has to pay to the IMF. In addition, a country is obligated to buy 195 WBG shares, of which about ½ % must be paid in cash in United States dollars and 5½ % can be paid in a country's local currency, in United States dollars, or in non-negotiable non-interest bearing notes. The balance of the 195 shares is left as callable capital, meaning the WBG reserves the right to ask for the monetary value of these shares when necessary. A country can subscribe for a further 250 shares, which do not require payment at the time of membership, but are left as callable capital.

The president of the World Bank comes from the largest shareholder, which is the United States, and members are represented by a Board of Governors. Powers are also delegated to a board of 24 executive directors (EDs). The five largest shareholders, the United States, Britain, France, Germany and Japan, each have an individual ED, and the additional 19 EDs represent the rest of the member states as groups of constituencies. Of these 19, however, China, Russia and Saudi Arabia have opted to be single country constituencies, and thus they each have one representative within the 19 EDs. These countries have large, influential economies, which requires that their interests be voiced individually rather than diluted within a group. Thus, the WBG gets its funding from rich countries as well as from the issuance of bonds on the world's capital markets.

The IBRD offers assistance to middle income and poor but credit worthy countries, and it also works as an umbrella for more specialized bodies under the WBG. The International Development Association offers loans to the world's poorest countries in the form of credits, and are essentially interest-free by having a 10-year grace period and holding a maturity of 35 years to 40 years.

Over time, it has been realized that sometimes as a poor nation develops, it requires more aid to work its way through the development process. This has resulted in some countries accumulating so much debt and debt service that payments become impossible to meet. Many of the poorest countries can receive accelerated debt relief through the Heavily Indebted Poor Countries scheme, which reduces debt and debt service payments while encouraging social expenditure. Another issue has presented itself as an endangerment to a country's livelihood, such as support programs for HIV/AIDS. Thus, the WBG has been focusing on reducing the risk of such projects by means of better appraisal and supervision mechanisms as well as a multidimensional approach to their overall development.

In 2015, the IDF added the Chinese yuan as one of its reserve currencies under the Special Drawing Rights (SDR) basket, thus challenging the preeminence of the United States dollar—as well as the other SDR reserve currencies that include the Japanese Yen, the British pound and the European Union euro.

The 21st Century

The early 2000s were marked by consolidation of existing banks and entrance into the market of other financial intermediaries, such as the non-bank financial institution. Large corporate players, such as insurance companies, found their way into the financial service community, offering competition to established banks. The services that were offered included insurance, pension, mutual, money market and hedge funds, loans, and credits and securities. By the end of 2001, the market capitalization of the world's 15 largest financial services providers included 4 non-banks.

The process of financial innovation advanced in the first decade of the 21st century increasing the importance and profitability of nonbank finance institutions. Such profitability that was restricted to the non-banking industry, prompted the Office of Comptroller of the Currency to encourage banks to explore other financial instruments, diversifying banks' business as well as improving banking economic health. As the distinct financial instruments were being explored and adopted by both the banking and non-banking industries, the distinction between different financial institutions became blurred. The first decade of the 21st century also saw the culmination of the technical innovation in banking over the previous 30 years and saw a major shift away from traditional banking to Internet banking.

The 2000s financial crisis caused significant stress on banks around the world. The failure of a large number of major banks resulted in government bail-outs. The government takeover of Fannie Mae and Freddie Mac, the federal bailout of American International Group, the collapse and sale of Bear Stearns and Washington Mutual to J. P. Morgan Chase, plus the collapse of Lehman Brothers led to a credit crunch and global banking crises. In response governments around the world bailed-out, nationalized or arranged sales for a large number of major banks. Governments around the world provided wholesale guarantees to underwriting banks to avoid the panic of systematic failure to the entire banking system. These events resulted in many discussions about the wisdom of these actions. Nevertheless, the United States Congress passed the Emergency Economic Stabilization Act, creating a $700,000,000,000 Treasury fund to purchase failing bank assets in a bailout of the financial system. The money was appropriated to purchase distressed assets, especially mortgage-backed securities, and to supply cash directly to banks.

Goldman-Sachs

The Goldman Sachs Group, Inc. is an American multinational finance company that engages in global investment banking, investment management, securities and other financial services, primarily with institutional clients. Goldman Sachs was founded in 1869 in New York City, New York by Marcus Goldman. In 1882, Goldman's son-in-law Samuel Sachs joined the firm. In 1885, Goldman took his son Henry and his son-in-law Ludwig Dreyfuss into the business and the firm adopted its present name, Goldman Sachs & Co. The company made a name for itself by pioneering the use of commercial paper for entrepreneurs. The company joined the NYSE in 1896, and by 1898, the firm's capital stood at $1,600,000. Goldman-Sachs entered the IPO market in 1906 when it took Sears, Roebuck and Company public. Other IPOs followed, including F. W. Woolworth and Continental Can.

In 1917, under growing pressure from the other partners in the firm due to his pro-German stance, Henry Goldman resigned. Control of the firm then fell to the Sachs family. In 1928, the firm launched the Goldman Sachs Trading Corp., a closed-end fund. The fund failed during the1929 crash, amid accusations that Goldman had engaged in share price manipulation and insider trading.

In 1930, Sidney Weinberg assumed the role of senior partner and shifted Goldman's focus away from trading towards investment banking. It was Weinberg's actions that helped to restore Goldman's reputation by being the lead advisor on the Ford Motor Company's IPO in 1956. Under Weinberg's reign the firm also started an investment research division and a municipal bond department, and also became an innovator in risk arbitrage.

Gus Levy joined the firm in the 1950s as a securities trader, which started a trend at Goldman of having one power from investment banking and another power from securities trading. For most of the 1950s and 1960s, the leaders would be Weinberg and Levy. Levy was a pioneer in block trading, with the firm establishing this trend under his guidance. Due to Weinberg's influence at the firm, it formed an investment banking division in 1956 in an attempt to spread around influence and not focus it all on Weinberg.

In 1969, Levy took over as Senior Partner, and built Goldman's trading franchise once again. It is Levy who is credited with Goldman's philosophy that as long as money is made over the long term, trading losses in the short term were not to be concerned with. Partners reinvested almost all of their earnings in the firm, so the focus was always on the future.

A financial crisis for the firm occurred in 1970, when the Penn Central Transportation Company went bankrupt with over $80,000,000 in commercial paper outstanding, most of it issued through Goldman Sachs. The bankruptcy was large, and the resulting lawsuits threatened the partnership capital, life and reputation of the firm. It was this bankruptcy that resulted in credit ratings being created for every issuer of commercial paper by credit rating services.

During the 1970s, the firm expanded in several ways. Under the direction of senior partner Stanley Miller, it opened its first international office in London in 1970, and created a private wealth division and a fixed income division in 1972. It pioneered the white knight strategy in 1974 during its attempts to defend Electric Storage Battery against a hostile takeover bid from International Nickel. This action boosted the firm's reputation as an investment advisor because it pledged to no longer participate in hostile takeovers.

John Weinberg and John Whitehead assumed the roles of co-senior partners in 1976, once again emphasizing the co-leadership at the firm. One of their initiatives was the establishment of 14 business principles that the firm applies:

1.   Our clients' interests always come first.

2.   Our assets are our people, capital and reputation.

3.   Our goal is to provide superior returns to our shareholders.

4.   We take great pride in the professional quality of our work.

5.   We stress creativity and imagination in everything we do.

6.   We make an unusual effort to identify and recruit the very best person for every job.

7.   We offer our people the opportunity to move ahead more rapidly than is possible at most other places.

8.   We stress teamwork in everything we do.

9.   The dedication of our people to the firm and the intense effort they give their jobs are greater than one finds in most other organizations.

10.   We consider our size an asset that we try hard to preserve.

11.   We constantly strive to anticipate the rapidly changing needs of our clients and to develop new services to meet those needs.

12.   We regularly receive confidential information as part of our normal client relationships.

13.   Our business is highly competitive, and we aggressively seek to expand our client relationships.

14.   Integrity and honesty are at the heart of our business.

In 1981, the firm acquired J. Aron & Company, a commodities trading firm, which merged with the fixed income division to become known as Fixed Income, Currencies, and Commodities, especially because J. Aron was a player in the coffee and gold markets. In 1985, the firm underwrote the public offering of the real estate investment trust that owned Rockefeller Center.

In 1986, the firm formed Goldman Sachs Asset Management, which manages the majority of its mutual funds and hedge funds. In 1986, the firm also underwrote the IPO of Microsoft, advised General Electric on its acquisition of RCA, and joined the London and Tokyo stock exchanges. In 1986, Goldman became the first United States bank to rank in the top 10 of mergers and acquisitions in Britain. During the 1980s the firm became the first bank to distribute its investment research electronically and created the first public offering of original issue deep-discount bonds.

Robert Rubin and Stephen Friedman assumed the Co-Senior Partnership in 1990 and pledged to focus on globalization of the firm and strengthening the Merger & Acquisition and Trading business lines. During their reign, the firm introduced paperless trading to the New York Stock Exchange and lead-managed the first-ever global debt offering by a United States corporation. It also launched the Goldman-Sachs Commodity Index and opened a Beijing office in 1994.

When the Soviet Union dissolved in 1991, the firm became involved in facilitating the global privatization movement by advising companies that were spinning off from their parent governments, such as the Soviet Union. Another event in Goldman's history was the Mexican bailout of 1995 when the 1994 economic crisis in Mexico threatened to wipe out the value of Mexico's bonds that were held by Goldman Sachs. Secretary of the Treasury Robert Rubin—a former senior partner of Goldman-Sachs—drew criticism from Congress for using a Treasury Department account under his personal control to distribute $20,000,000,000 to bail out Mexican bonds, of which Goldman-Sachs was the key distributor that was operating in that market.

The firm joined David Rockefeller and partners in a 50–50 joint ownership of Rockefeller Center during 1994, but later sold the shares in 2000. In 1996, Goldman was lead underwriter of the Yahoo! IPO and in 1998 it was global coordinator of the NTT DoCoMo IPO.

During the 2007 subprime mortgage crisis, Goldman-Sachs was able to profit from the collapse in subprime mortgage bonds in the summer of 2007 by short-selling subprime mortgage-backed securities. Two Goldman traders, Michael Swenson and Josh Birnbaum, are credited with being responsible for the firm's large profits during the crisis. The pair made a profit of $4,000,000,000 by betting on a collapse in the sub-prime market, and shorting mortgage-related securities. By summer 2007, they persuaded colleagues to see their point of view and convinced skeptical risk management executives. The firm initially avoided large subprime write downs, and achieved a net profit due to significant losses on non-prime securitized loans being offset by gains on short mortgage positions. The firm's viability was later called into question as the crisis intensified in 2008, especially as backing by ultra-risky second-mortgage loans facilitated the housing bubble and bust. Due to its involvement in these subprime mortgages, Goldman-Sachs was hit hard by the 2008 economic crisis, and was subsequently rescued as part of a massive government bailout.

In 2008, Goldman Sachs and Morgan Stanley both confirmed that they would become traditional bank holding companies, bringing an end to the era of investment banking on Wall Street. The Federal Reserve's approval of their bid to become banks ended the ascendancy of the securities firms, and sent Lehman Brothers into bankruptcy, leading to the sale of Merrill Lynch & Co. to the Bank of America. Thus, the Goldman-Sachs' reputation suffered in 2008 and 2009. In 2008, Berkshire Hathaway agreed to purchase $5,000,000,000 in Goldman's preferred stock, and received warrants to buy another $5,000,000,000 of Goldman's common stock. Goldman also received a $10,000,000,000 preferred stock investment from the Treasury in 2008, as part of the Troubled Asset Relief Program (TARP).

In 2013, Goldman Sachs Group Inc. together with Deutsche Bank led Apple's largest corporate-bond deal in Apple Inc.'s history of a $17,000,000,000 offering that was the largest bond sale on record. In 2013, Goldman Sachs was the lead underwriter for Twitter's IPO. In 2015, Goldman Sachs agreed to acquire General Electric Company's GE Capital Bank on-line deposit platform, with the transaction including $8,000,000,000 of on-line deposits and another $8,000,000,000 of brokered certificates of deposit. In 2016, Goldman Sachs launched an online-only savings bank and started offering no-fee personal loans.

In spite of all the financial events and oftentimes bad press, some of the top executives have nevertheless been picked by Presidents to serve in the government. Former Goldman-Sachs executives who have served in government positions include the following:

Under President Franklin Roosevelt:

- Assistant Director of the War Production Board Sidney Weinberg

Under President Lyndon Johnson:

- Secretary of the Treasury Henry Fowler

Under President William Clinton:

- Secretary of the Treasury Robert Rubin
- Secretary of the Treasury Lawrence Summers
- Assistant Secretary for Financial Markets Gary Gensler
- President of the Export-Import Bank Kenneth Brody

Under President George W. Bush:

- White House Chief of Staff Joshua Bolten
- Under Secretary of State for Economic, Business and Agricultural Affairs Reuben Jeffery III
- Assistant Secretary of the Treasury for Financial Stability Neel Kashkari
- Secretary of the Treasury Henry Paulson
- White House Chief Economic Adviser Stephen Friedman

- Under Secretary of the Treasury Robert Steel

Under President Barack Obama:

- Chief of Staff to the Secretary of the Treasury Mark Patterson
- President of the Federal Reserve Bank William Dudley

Under President Donald Trump:

- Chief Strategist to the President Steve Bannon
- Director of the National Economic Council Gary Cohn
- Secretary of the Treasury Steven Mnuchin
- Deputy Treasury Secretary James Donovan
- Deputy National Security Adviser for Strategy Dina Powell

The company includes 4 businesses units: investment banking, institutional client services, investment management and the acquisition of businesses from Deutsche Bank. The current CEO of Goldman is Lloyd Blankfein. The firm provides asset management, mergers and acquisitions advice, prime brokerage and underwriting services to its clients—which includes corporations, governments, and individuals. The firm also engages in market making and private equity deals, and is a primary dealer in the Treasury security market. Goldman Sachs is everywhere and is the world's most powerful investment bank. In the history of financial crises, there are several significant episodes in which there were have been many losers—but Goldman Sachs has never been one of them. These events are as follows:

- The Great Depression
- Tech stocks boom and bust
- The housing mortgage debacle
- Gasoline price hike
- The Great Recession and bailout
- Global warming investments
- The food price rise

World's Oldest Banks

Three of the oldest banks in the world are still in operation today: the Banca Monte del Paschi di Siena, the Berenberg Bank and the Sveriges Riksbank.

<u>Banca Monte del Paschi di Siena</u>

Banca Monte dei Paschi di Siena (BMPS) is the oldest surviving bank in the world, and the third largest Italian commercial and retail bank by total assets. However, since 2016, BMPS has been struggling to avoid a collapse. Founded in 1472 by the magistrates of the city state of Siena, Italy, it has been operating ever since. In 1995, the bank, was transformed to a limited company called Banca Monte dei Paschi di Siena (Banca MPS). Also, a foundation was created to continue the charitable functions of the bank and to be, until the bailout in 2013, its largest single shareholder. Today BMPS has approximately 2,000 branches, 26,000 employees and 5,100,000 customers in Italy, as well as branches and businesses abroad.

The bank consolidated and increased its banking activity during the 17th and 18th centuries. The bank expanded its business throughout Italy initiating new activities, including mortgage loans. In 1999, BMPS was listed on the Italian Stock Exchange. The bank acquired some regional banks and absorbed a subsidiary. The bank also started a process to reinforce the structures of production in strategic market segments through the development of product companies.

The bank upgraded its commercial productivity, with the aim of improving the level of assistance and consultancy to investors and businesses, and updated its activities in private banking and private pension plans. The bank also opened more than 2,000 branches. To finance the expansion, the bank entered into some derivatives operations in 2006.

During the financial crisis that started in 2008, the bank suffered huge losses beginning in 2009, and lost over $2,000,000,000 in 2012, had to recapitalize, and faced restructuring or bankruptcy. The majority owner resisted issuing new capital which would dilute its holding. In 2012, even after the dilution, the bank appeared poised to give the national government a greater ownership stake in return for more capital.

In 2013, a meeting of the shareholders of the bank was convened. They resolved to grant the Board of Directors the power to increase the share capital by a maximum amount of 4,500,000,000 euros to service the exercise of conversion rights of the bank of its bonds. BMPS called for an intervention, and in 2013, the Bank of Italy approved a bailout request from the BMPS bank for 3.900,000,000 euros.

In 2014, the BMPS failed the European Central Bank's stress test of major European banks, and the bank was declared as being not able to withstand a financial catastrophe. Shares fell by 22% and the bank reported a loss of almost 1,150,000,000 euros, with an eventual financial year loss of almost 5,350,000,000 euros. In 2016, the European Union bank stress test was announced, and among the 51 banks in the test, BMPS was the only bank that was forecast as negative. In 2017, BMPS issued bonds with a 7,000,000,000 euros face value. The bonds would mature from 1 to 3 years, with the state guarantee from the government fund. The bank said the bond would be sold to the market or used as a collateral in borrowing. In 2017, BMPS sold its card business. In 2017, The European Commissioner agreed in-principle for the state aid of the bank, and the industrial plan of the bank was approved.

The Berenberg Bank

The Berenberg Bank is a multinational investment banking and private banking company founded by the Belgian Berenberg family. It is the world's oldest merchant bank and the world's second oldest bank. The bank was founded by Hans and Paul Berenberg in 1590 in Hamburg, Germany although they were originally from Antwerp, Belgium. The bank has been continuously owned by their descendants ever since. Hans Berenberg's grandson Coenelius Berenberg was the first to engage in merchant banking, and developed the company into a very successful merchant house and merchant bank. He forged trade links with France, Spain, Portugal, Italy, Scandinavia and Russia. Family connections of the Berenbergs led to the development in Livorno, Italy and Lisbon, Portugal with wealthy Dutch merchants in the 17th century.

By the mid 18th century, investment banking and acceptance credits comprised a significant part of the firm's activities. In the 19th century, the bank financed the industrialization process and transportation activities, and was strongly involved in the North American trade and its finance. The company was the main founders of the Norddeutsche Bank in 1856, the first joint-stock bank in northern Germany and one of the predecessors of Deutsche Bank. Berenberg Bank was also among the founding shareholders of Bergens Privatbank in 1855, the Hongkong and Shanghai Banking Corporation in 1865, The Den Danske Landmandsbank in 1871 and the Svenska Handelsbanken in 1871.

In recent years Berenberg's London office has become its second largest office, focusing on investment banking and private banking for the ultra-wealthy. The Berenberg Bank is active in investment banking, particularly European equity research, brokerage and capital markets transactions and institutional asset management. Berenberg Bank has around 1,500 employees with its headquarters located in Hamburg, Germany. It also has presences in England and the United States, and 11 offices in Europe, the Americas and Asia. The bank is organized as a limited partnership, and is noted for its conservative business strategy. Following the financial crisis of the 2000s, the bank has grown rapidly.

Sveriges Riksbank

Sveriges Riksbank is the central bank of Sweden. It is the world's oldest central bank and the third oldest bank still in operation. The Riksbank began operations in 1668 when the privilege to operate a bank was given to the Riksens Standers Bank run under the auspices of the parliament of the day. The bank was managed under the direct control of the Riksdag of the Estates to prevent the interference from the king. When a new Riksdag was instituted in 1866, the name of the bank was changed to Sveriges Riksbank.

The Riksbank was not permitted to issue bank-notes. Nevertheless, in 1701, permission was granted to issue credit notes. In the mid-18th century, counterfeit notes began appearing, which caused serious problems. To prevent forgeries, the Riksbank produced its own paper for bank notes and a paper mill was established on the outskirts of Stockholm. When the first commercial banks were founded, these were also allowed to issue bank notes. The bank notes represented a claim to the bank without interest paid, and thus became a considerable source of income for banks. Nonetheless, security in the form of a deposit at the Riksbank was required to cover the value of all banknotes that were issued.

During the 19th century, the Riksbank maintained a dominant position as a credit institution and issuer of bank notes. The bank also managed national trade transactions as well as continuing to provide credit to the general public. The first branch office was opened in 1824, followed with subsidiary branches opening in each county.

Riksbank as a central bank dates back to 1897, when the first Riksbank Act was accepted concurrently with a law giving the Riksbank the exclusive right to issue bank notes in order to conduct monetary policy and defend the value of a currency. The Swedish currency was backed by gold and the paper certificates could be exchanged for gold coins until 1931, when a specialized temporary law freed the bank from this obligation. This law was renewed every year until the new constitution was ratified in 1975, which split the bank from the government into a standalone organization not obligated to exchange notes for gold.

From 1991 to 1993, Sweden experienced its most severe recession. In 1992, the fixed exchange rate of the Swedish Krona collapsed. In 1993, the Governing Board of the Riksbank developed a new monetary policy based on a floating exchange rate. Thus, it forced inflation down to around 2%, which continued to be low during the years of strong growth in the late 1990s. During the 2000s, the operations and administrative departments were downsized, and a direct consequence was that the Riksbank closed down all its branches in Sweden and outsourced the handling of coins and bills to a private company. Today the policy departments are the core of the central bank and they employ about half of the bank's 350 fulltime posts.

In 2009, Riksbank was the first central bank in the world to implement a negative interest rate. This caused its deposit rate to be pushed down to –0.25%. This was done to counter economic slowdown due to the financial crisis of 2008. The Swedish move to a negative discount rate was followed with great interest by central banks around the world. In 2014, Riksbank cut its repo rate to 0.00%, which pushed the linked deposit rate to –0.75%. In 2015, the repo rate was lowered again, to –0.10%. The deposit rate was then lowered to –0.85%. Riksbank cut the repo rate even more to -0.25%. Since that time, the deposit rate has been lowered to –1.00%. Riksbank has consequently lowered the rate two more times, and the accompanying deposit rate now lies at -1.25.

The World's Largest Banks

Because of the growth of economies in the world, several banks have emerged that are huge in terms of assets and equity that they own. The four largest banks are those of China, with the fifth largest being that of Japan. The highest that the United States ranks is sixth with the J. P. Morgan Chase & Co. Bank. China has 19 of the top 100 banks, the United States has 10, Japan has 9, France has 7, Britain, Germany and South Korea have 6 each, Canada and Brazil have 5 each, Australia has 4, Switzerland has 2, and Spain and India have 1 each.

The top 23 banks in the world are as follows:

1. Industrial and Commerce Bank of China

    This is the largest bank in the world by total assets and the most valuable bank in the world by market capitalization. The bank was founded in 1984, and as of 2015 had assets and equity that were worth $3,616,000,000,000. It has an annual revenue of over $725,000,000,000 and an annual profit of over $125,000,000,000. It offers banking, financial and investment services. Its headquarters are in Beijing, China.

2. China Construction Bank Corporation

    This is the second largest bank with respect to market capitalization. The bank has over 13,625 domestic branches as well as branches in Spain, Germany, Luxemburg, South Africa, South Korea, the United States, Japan, Singapore, Australia and New Zealand. The bank was founded in 1954, and has assets worth $3,018,000,000,000. It has almost $400,000,000,000 in revenue yearly, and employs almost 330,000 employees. Its headquarters are in Beijing, China.

3. Agricultural Bank of China

    This bank is China's third largest lender by assets. The bank has almost 24,000 branches in China, with branches also in Britain, Japan, the United States, Germany, Australia, South korea and Singapore. The bank was founded in 1951, and has assets worth $2,817,000,000,000.
    Its headquarters are in Beijing, China. It has over $420,000,000,000 in revenue yearly, and employs over 444,000 employees. In 2010, it went public with the world's biggest ever IPO.

4. Bank of China

    The Bank of China is one of the 5 biggest state-owned commercial banks in China. It was founded in 1912 to replace the *Daqing* Bank. It is the oldest bank in mainland China still in existence. From its establishment until 1942, it issued banknotes on behalf of the

Government. Its headquarters are in Beijing. As of 2009, it was the second largest lender in China, and the 5th largest bank in the world by market capitalization value. It is the most globally-active of China's banks, with branches on every continent. It operates in 27 countries, including Australia, Canada, the United Kingdom, Ireland, France, Germany, Italy, Luxembourg, Russia, Hungary, United States, Panama, Brazil, Japan, South Korea, Singapore, Taiwan, the Philippines, Vietnam, Malaysia, Thailand, Indonesia, Kazakhstan, Bahrain, Zambia, South Africa and the Cayman Islands.

5. Mitsubishi UFJ Financial Group

Mitsubishi UFJ Financial Group, Inc. (MUFG) is a Japanese bank holding and financial services company that is headquartered in Tokyo, Japan. MUFG holds assets of almost $2,500,000,000,000 as of 2016, making it the world's fourth largest bank by total assets. It is Japan's largest financial group and the world's second largest bank holding company holding around $1,800,000,000,000 in deposits. MUFG is the second largest public company in Japan in terms of market capitalization. The company was formed in 2005 with the merger of Mitsubishi Tokyo Financial Group and the UFJ Holdings Bank.

6. J. P. Morgan Chase & Co.

JP Morgan Chase & Co. is a U.S. multinational banking and financial services holding company that is headquartered in New York City, New York. It is the largest bank in the United States, and the world's third largest bank by total assets of $2,500,000,000,000 and is the world's most valuable bank by market capitalization. It is a major provider of financial services, and is the world's sixth largest public company. The hedge fund unit of JP Morgan Chase is the second largest hedge fund in the United States. The company was formed in 2000, when Chase Manhattan Corporation merged with JP Morgan & Co. As of 2016, JP Morgan Chase is one of the big four banks of the United States, followed by Bank of America, Citigroup and Wells Fargo.

7. HSBC Holdings PLC

HSBC Holdings PLC is a British–Hong Kong multinational banking and financial services holding company headquartered in London, England. It is the world's seventh largest bank by total assets, and the largest in Europe with total assets of almost $2,375,000,000,000 . It was established in London, England in 1991 by the Hong Kong and Shanghai Banking Corporation Limited, the origins of which were first opened in 1865. HSBC has around 4,000 offices in 70 countries across Africa, Asia,

Oceania, Europe, North America and South America, and around 37,000,000 customers. It is the world's sixth-largest public company.

8. BNP Paribas

BNP Paribas is an international banking group with a presence in 75 countries. Its net income in 2016 was 7,702,000,000 euros. The bank serves more than 30,000,000 customers between its retail banking networks in France, Belgium, Italy and Luxembourg. The retail bank also operates in the Mediterranean region and in the United States. The bank was formed through the merger of Banque Nationale de Paris (BNP) and Paribas in 2000. BNP Paribas was the second leading bank in Europe in 2016 and was ranked fifth internationally. It has its headquarters in Paris, France.

9. Bank of America

Bank of America Corporation is a multinational banking and financial services corporation headquartered in Charlotte, North Carolina. It is the second largest bank in the United States by assets, and the eleventh largest company in the world. Its acquisition of Merrill Lynch in 2008 made it the world's largest wealth management corporation and a major player in the investment banking market. As of 2016, it had $886,148,000,000 in assets and held almost 11% of all bank deposits in the United States. Bank of America operates in more than 40 other countries, and serves 46,000,000 consumer and small business relationships at 4,600 banking centers.

10. Wells Fargo & Co.

Wells Fargo & Company is an American international banking and financial services holding company that is headquartered in San Francisco, California. It is the world's second-largest bank by market capitalization and the third largest bank in the United States by assets. In 2015, Wells Fargo became the world's largest bank by market capitalization, edging past China's ICBC before slipping behind JP Morgan Chase in 2016. Wells Fargo surpassed Citigroup Inc. to become the third-largest United States bank by assets at the end of 2015. Wells Fargo is the second-largest bank in deposits, home mortgage servicing, and debit cards. Wells Fargo is a result of a merger between Wells Fargo & Company and the Norwest Corporation in 1998 and the subsequent 2008 acquisition of Wachovia. It has 8,700 retail branches and operates across 35 countries, with over 70,000,000 customers.

11. Credit Agricole

Credit Agricole is a French network of cooperative and mutual banks comprising the 39 Credit Agricole Regional Banks. In 1990, it became an international full-service banking group. In 2013, the Credit Agricole Group reported revenues of 26,400,000,000 euros. It has 7,400,000 stakeholders who are both clients and owners of the share capital. Credit Agricole can trace its history back to the Act of 1884 establishing the freedom of professional association, which authorized the creation of farm unions and the foundation of local mutual banks. Societe de Credit Agricole was created in 1885. Its headquarters are in Paris, France.

12. Japan Post Bank

Japan Post Bank is a Japanese bank that is headquartered in Tokyo. It is part of the Japan Post Holdings postal and financial services group, and is the world's biggest deposit holder. It has branches in every prefecture in Japan. The bank was established in 2006 as part of the reorganization of Japan Post into Japan Post Holdings.

13. Citigroup Inc.

Citigroup Inc. is an American multinational investment banking and financial services corporation that is headquartered in New York City, New York. The company was formed by the merger of Citicorp and Travelers Group in 1998; however, Travelers Group was spun off from the company in 2002. Citigroup now owns Citicorp, the holding company for Citibank and several international subsidiaries, Citigroup is the 4th largest bank in the United States by assets, and has over 200,000,000 customer accounts, doing business in more than 160 countries. Citigroup has 230,000 employees. Citigroup suffered huge losses during the financial crisis of 2008, and was rescued as part of a massive stimulus package by the government.

14. Mizuho Financial Group

Mizuho Financial Group is a banking holding company that is headquartered in Tokyo, Japan. It holds assets of $1,600,000,000,000 through its control of Mizuho Bank, Mizuho Corporate Bank and subsidiaries. The company's combined holdings form the second largest financial services group in Japan. Its banking businesses rank 3rd in Japan and 13th in the world by total assets. Mizuho employs more than 56,000 people in 900 offices, and serves over 26,000,000 Japanese households. Mizuho was established by the merger of Dai-Ichi Kangyo Bank, Fuji Bank and the Industrial Bank of Japan in 2000.

15. Deutsche Bank

Deutsche Bank is a German global banking and financial services company, with its headquarters in Frankfurt, Germany. Deutsche Bank was founded in 1870 as a specialist bank for foreign trade. It has more than 100,000 employees in over 70 countries, and has a large presence in Europe, the Americas and Asia-Pacific. In 2009, Deutsche Bank was the largest foreign exchange dealer in the world with a market share of 21%. Deutsche Bank's core business is investment banking, which represents 50% of equity, 75% of leverage assets and 50% of profits. In 2014, Deutsche Bank reported a 1,200,000,000 euro loss for the fourth quarter of 2013, with revenues slipping by 16%. In 2016, Deutsche Bank announced a 2015 net loss of approximately 6,700,000,000 euros.

16. Sumitomo Mitsui Financial Group

Sumitomo Mitsui Financial Group is a Japanese bank holding and financial services company that was established by Sumitomo Mitsui Banking Corporation in 2002 through a share transfer. The bank is headquartered in Tokyo, Japan and has over 62,000 employees. It holds assets of around $1.800,000,000,000 and is one of the largest financial institutions in the world. In 2016, it acquired General Electric's leasing business in Japan.

17. Barclays PLC

Barclays PLC is a British multinational bank and financial service company that is headquartered in London, England. It is a transatlantic consumer, corporate and investment bank with global reach, offering products and services across personal, corporate and investment banking, credit cards and wealth management, with a strong presence in its two home markets of Britain and the United States. It has operations in over 40 countries and employs approximately 120,000 people. Barclays traces its origins to a goldsmith banking business established in London in 1690. In 1896, several banks in London and the English provinces united as a joint-stock bank under the name Barclays and Co. Over the following decades Barclays expanded to become a nationwide bank. In 1967, Barclays made numerous corporate acquisitions, including the North American operations of Lehman Brothers in 2008. Barclays is the most powerful transnational corporation in terms of ownership, and thus has corporate control over global financial stability and market competition.

18. Societe Generale

Societe Generale is a French multinational banking and financial services company that is headquartered in Paris, France. The company is a universal bank and has divisions supporting other banking services. Societe Generale is France's 3rd largest bank by total assets and the 6th largest in Europe. Societe Generale is one of the oldest banks in France, and was founded in 1864.

19. Banco Santander

The Santander Group is a Spanish banking group. The group has expanded since 2000 through a number of acquisitions, with operations across Europe, Latin America, North America and Asia. Many subsidiaries have been rebranded under the Santander name. Banco Santander was founded in 1857. In 1999, it merged with Banco Central Hispano. it has more than 186,000 employees, 14,392 branches, 3,260,000 shareholders and 102,000,000 customers. Its headquarters are in Madrid, Spain.

20. Groupe BPCE

Groupe BPCE is France's second largest bank, which was formed by the 2009 merger of CNCE and BFBP. It has more than 8,200 branches nationwide serving nearly 40,000,000 customers. It provides banking, financial, and real estate financing services to individuals, professionals, small, medium and large enterprises, and institutions in France and internationally. In 2016, the group announced the purchase of Fidor Bank that was operating in Britain and Germany.

21. Bank of Communications

The Bank of Communications was founded in 1908, and has a long history in China. It is one of the banks to have issued banknotes in modern Chinese history. It is headquartered in Shanghai, China. The bank was restructured in 1986, and today is one of the five leading commercial banks in China. It possesses 12 branch banks in Hong Kong and Macau, China; New York City and San Francisco in the United States; Tokyo, Japan; Singapore; Seoul, South Korea Frankfurt, Germany; Sydney, Australia; and Ho Chi Minh City, Vietnam.

22. Postal Savings Bank of China

The Postal Savings Bank of China (PSBC) is a commercial retail bank, which provides financial services, especially to small to medium enterprises to rural and low income customers. PSBC has 40,000 branches covering all regions of China. PSBC was set up in 2007 from the State Post Bureau. Today it has the second largest number of branches, after the Agricultural Bank of China. During the Global Financial Crisis of 2008, the government took several measures to spread its national economic stimulus plan specifically to rural areas. The bank is headquartered in Beijing, China.

23. Lloyds Banking Group

Lloyds Banking Group is a British financial institution formed through the acquisition of HBOS by Lloyds TSB in 2009. The Group's history stems from the founding in 1695 by the Parliament of Scotland of the Bank of Scotland, which is the second oldest bank in the United Kingdom. The Group's headquarters is located in London, England. Lloyds Banking Group's activities are organized into Retail Banking, Commercial, Life, Pensions & Insurance and Wealth & International. Lloyds' has extensive overseas operations in the United States, Europe, the Middle East and Asia. Lloyds Banking Group has a market capitalization of 57,700,000,000 British pounds.

The Future of Banking

With a $20,000,000,000,000 national debt in the United States, a sharp economic decline could cause banking corporations to fail on a massive scale, but probably the government would bail out those which are most inefficient. However, there exist very complex derivatives contracts that one financial institution owes another who then sells it on to the next and again sells it on to the next one in a daisy chain fashion. Thus, if just one of these institutions can't make a payment, the next bank then can't make a payment also, and then continues to the next bank, and so on.

In 2010, the Federal Reserve stated that they couldn't possibly come up with the assets to bail out the banking institutions because there is much more debt existing in the world. Thus, the United States is in a very dangerous situation from a financial, economic, sociological and political position because the monetary system is unstable—even though it is the world's top reserve currency. Zero and negative interest rates will not help, and printing more dollars will only create more inflation.

One alternative that is being considered by the Federal Reserve is something similar to the Bitcoin. This is the blockchain technology where every transaction can be tracked from the creation of the Bitcoin itself. A completely digital currency will actually act as a parallel and alternative to the dollar. It will have a lot of advantages in that it will not be based on paper currency. Hence, it will exist on smartphones—with access by fingerprints—or even on chips implanted in human beings, which will also have additional information such as medical records. As an indicator of where this is heading, Goldman Sachs filed a patent application for a virtual currency in 2014. Also, company apps like Apple's Applepay, PayPal's Venmo and Square Cash are increasingly being used for payments of all types.

Digital money will result in a cashless society. This will eliminate many of the ills that currently exist with a cash economy, such as tax evasion, underground transactions, drug exchanges, and money laundering. The presence of transparency with blockchain technology allows everything to be seen everywhere, so that no privacy will exist. The Federal Reserve System will know exactly what you are buying and selling as well as how much you are earning. It also ensures them that you are going to pay your taxes. Moreover, there is the possibility that an element of control can be instituted in such a system via programming as to where the digital money can be spent—and what it can be spent on. More importantly, banks cannot run out of money because *there is no money* since it is all computerized. If a scheme like this materializes, then we could see the end of our economic freedom as we know it—and, more dangerous, other freedoms as well.

Bibliography

De Roover, Raymond Adrien. *The Rise and Decline of the Medici Bank: 1397-1494*. New York City: W. W. Norton & Company, Inc., 1966.

Endlich, Lisa. *Goldman Sachs: The Culture of Success*. New York: A. A. Knopf, 1999.

Elon, Amos. *Founder: Meyer Amschel Rothschild and His Time*. New York: HarperCollins, 1996.

Goodson, Stephen Milford. *A History of Central Banking and the Enslavement of Mankind.* London: Black House Publishing, Ltd., 2014.

Griffin, G. Edward. *The Creature from Jekyll Island: A Second Look at the Federal Reserve.* New York City: American Media, 2010.

Hibbert, Christopher. *The House of Medici: Its Rise and Fall.* New York: William Morrow and Company, 1975.

Hoggson, N. F. *Banking Through the Ages.* New York: Dodd, Mead & Company, 1926.

http://www.businessinsider.com/the-biggest-banks-in-the-world-2017-4?r=UK&IR=T/#3-agricultural-bank-of-china-china-282-trillion-21.

Kynaston, David. *Till Time's Last Stand: A History of the Bank of England, 1694-2013.* New York City: Bloomsbury Publishing, 2017.

LeBor, Adam. *Tower of Basel: The Shadowy History of the Secret Bank that Runs the World*. New York City: Public Affairs, 2014.

Manfred Pohl and Sabine Freitag, *Handbook on the History of European Banks*. Frankfurt: European Association for Banking History, 1994

Vreeland, James Raymond. *The International Monetary Fund: Politics of Conditional Lending*. Florence: Routledge, 2006.

Woods, Roger and Michael J. Lafferty. *Bank Annual Reports: 1992 World Survey - An Analysis of the Annual Reports of 100 of the World's Largest Banks, Drawn from 28 Countries.* London: Lafferty Publications LTD, 1992.

www.ingramcontent.com/pod-product-compliance
Lightning Source LLC
Chambersburg PA
CBHW080138240526
45468CB00009BA/2522